A Beginner's Guide to New Brunswick's Car Accident Compensation System

Learn What You Need to Know to Protect Your Right to Fair Compensation

DAVID BRANNEN

Copyright © 2013 David Brannen.

All rights reserved. No part of this book may be reproduced, stored, or transmitted by any means—whether auditory, graphic, mechanical, or electronic—without written permission of both publisher and author, except in the case of brief excerpts used in critical articles and reviews. Unauthorized reproduction of any part of this work is illegal and is punishable by law.

ISBN: 978-1-4834-0359-5 (sc)
ISBN: 978-1-4834-0358-8 (e)

Because of the dynamic nature of the Internet, any web addresses or links contained in this book may have changed since publication and may no longer be valid. The views expressed in this work are solely those of the author and do not necessarily reflect the views of the publisher, and the publisher hereby disclaims any responsibility for them.

Any people depicted in stock imagery provided by Thinkstock are models, and such images are being used for illustrative purposes only.
Certain stock imagery © Thinkstock.

Lulu Publishing Services rev. date: 9/30/2013

Table of Contents

Introduction vii

Chapter 1   The Big Picture: New Brunswick's Compensation System for Vehicle Accidents 1

Chapter 2   Making a Claim for Your Damaged Vehicle 5

Chapter 3   Making a Claim for No-Fault Accident Benefits 12

Chapter 4   Making a Claim for Personal Injury Compensation 19

Chapter 5   "Minor Personal Injury" Claims 29

Chapter 6   Representing Yourself 33

Chapter 7   The Ten Things You Must Do in the First Two Weeks after Your Accident 39

Chapter 8   Ten Mistakes That Will Ruin Your Injury Claim 45

Chapter 9   Common Scenarios: What You Need to Do 51

Introduction

The moment you were in a vehicle accident, you instantly became a player in New Brunswick's car accident compensation system. You are now part of a complex system where everyone *(except for you)* knows how the game is played. Everyone *(except for you)* knows how to tip the odds in their favour. Your lack of knowledge puts you at a major disadvantage.

This is why learning how the system *really* works is the first thing you need to do: Before you meet with any insurance representatives. Before you sign any forms. Before you hire a lawyer.

A Beginner's Guide to New Brunswick's Car Accident Compensation System is for people who want to learn how the system *really* works. You will learn the steps—from start to finish—for getting the insurance benefits and compensation you need for financial security. You will learn what you need to do to protect your own interests. You will learn the most common mistakes people make and how you can avoid them.

I have organized the book into nine chapters. Start with Chapter 1, but then read the other chapters in any order.

Chapter 1 gives an overview of New Brunswick's vehicle accident compensation system, including the types of accidents that are covered and the three claims you can make.

Chapter 2 explains how you get your vehicle repaired or replaced after the accident. I give step-by-step instruction on what you need to do.

Chapter 3 reviews important insurance benefits available to anyone injured in a vehicle accident.

Chapter 4 explains how to know if you are eligible to make a claim for injury compensation, and how to get started on your own, or with a lawyer.

Chapter 5 reviews *minor personal injury* claims, including how to know if your case may qualify as a minor injury case.

Chapter 6 explains the things you need to consider when deciding whether to handle your own insurance claims or to hire a lawyer to do it for you.

Chapter 7 outlines the ten things you must do in the first two weeks following your accident.

Chapter 8 reviews the ten common mistakes that will ruin your car accident injury claim.

Finally, Chapter 9 includes three common vehicle accident scenarios and explains what you should do in each situation.

Now that you know where we are going, lets get started!

CHAPTER 1

The Big Picture: New Brunswick's Compensation System for Vehicle Accidents

In this chapter:

- overview of the system
- situations that are covered
- three claims you can make

Overview of the System

Each year thousands of people are involved in vehicle accidents in New Brunswick. Several thousand accidents result in minor to severe injuries, and up to a hundred accidents result in deaths. This makes vehicle accidents the one of the leading cause of injury in New Brunswick. Vehicle accidents include those involving cars, motorcycles, trucks, ATVs, snowmobiles, and pedestrians struck by any of these vehicles. Because so many people are hurt, New Brunswick, like all other provinces in Canada, has a special compensation system for vehicle accidents.

New Brunswick has an insurance-based compensation system that is made up of three parts: 1) vehicle damage compensation, 2) no-fault accident benefits, and 3) personal injury compensation. With parts 1 and 2 (vehicle damage and accident benefits), you seek compensation or benefits by filing a claim with an insurance company. With part 3 (personal injury compensation), you seek compensation by filing a lawsuit against the person at fault for the accident.

You trigger the compensation system by filing a claim with the insurance company (for property damage or accident benefits) or by filing a lawsuit (personal injury compensation) with the court. Once you file a claim or lawsuit, it is up to the insurance company to accept or reject your claim (vehicle damage or accident benefits) or to offer you an out-of-court settlement (personal injury compensation).

You deal directly with insurance company's representatives (called "adjusters"). The courts have the power to resolve all disputes between you and your insurance company. If you can't reach an out-of-court settlement with your insurance company, then a judge will have the final say on how much, if any, compensation or benefits your insurance company must pay you. Decisions of the judge or are legally binding on both you and your insurance company.

What Situations and Vehicle Accidents Are Covered?

New Brunswick's compensation system applies to all motorized vehicles, including cars, trucks, motorcycles, off-highway vehicles (OHVs), all-terrain vehicles (ATVs), and snowmobiles. You can make a claim for accident benefits or personal injury compensation if you are hurt in accidents involving any of these vehicles. This includes pedestrians or bicyclists hit by any of the above vehicles.

The Three Claims You Can Make

After being involved in a vehicle accident, you can make three possible claims. You can make a claim for 1) vehicle damage compensation, 2) no-fault accident benefits, and 3) personal injury compensation. Things get a bit complicated because you usually don't make all three claims with the same insurance company (but sometimes you do). Following is an overview of each claim.

Claim for Vehicle Damage Compensation

If your vehicle is damaged in an accident, you may have the right to make a claim for the cost of repairs or for the actual cash value of your vehicle if it is damaged beyond repair. With very limited exceptions, you always make your vehicle damage claim with your own insurance company, regardless of who was at fault for the accident.

You make the claim by notifying your insurance company that your vehicle was damaged. You will need to fill out paperwork and forms for your insurance company. If your insurance company agrees that another driver was at fault, it will pay compensation to you and seek reimbursement from the at-fault driver's insurance company.

There is one exception. If you or the other driver was in a non-New Brunswick registered vehicle, then you need to make your property damage claim directly with the at-fault driver's insurance company.

Claim for No-Fault Accident Benefits

With very limited exceptions, everyone hurt in a car accident is entitled to make a claim for no-fault accident benefits. The reference to "no-fault" means that these benefits are available to everyone, regardless of fault.

No-fault accident benefits include reimbursement for medical expenses and a monthly disability payment for loss of income. You can make a no-fault benefits claim to cover medical expenses for private rehabilitation with physiotherapists, massage therapists, chiropractors, or for other treatments recommended by your doctor. You can also claim reimbursement for accident-related medical expenses for things like prescription drugs, medical devices, or ambulance bills. If your injuries prevent you from returning to work, then you can apply for weekly disability income payments for up to $250 per week.

If you were a driver or passenger in a car, then you make your no-fault benefits claim with the insurance policy covering the car you were in. If you were a pedestrian or bicyclist hit by a car, then you make your no-fault benefits claim under that car's insurance policy. The only time you don't qualify to make a claim for no-fault accident benefits is if you were in violation of the terms of the insurance policy. Common violations are driving while intoxicated or driving a car without the owner's permission.

Claim for Personal Injury Compensation

If you are injured in a car accident and another person was at fault for the accident, then you have the right to make a claim for personal injury compensation. Once you give notice of your intention to make a claim, the at-fault driver's insurance company will step in to investigate and defend against your claim.

Personal injury claims are different than claims for vehicle damage or accident benefits. You don't make a personal injury claim by filing forms with the insurance company; rather, you start a personal injury claim by notifying the insurance company of your intention to file a personal injury lawsuit with the New Brunswick Court of Queen's Bench.

In most cases, you will have two years from the date of the accident to file your lawsuit for injury compensation. In the meantime, you can try to negotiate an out-of-court settlement with the negligent driver's insurance company. If you can't reach a settlement, then your case would go to trial before a judge, and he or she would decide how much compensation (if any) the insurance company must pay you.

CHAPTER 2

Making a Claim for Your Damaged Vehicle

In this chapter:

- vehicle damage that is covered by insurance
- how to know if you qualify to make a claim
- vehicle damage claims: four steps from start to finish
- disputes over actual cash value

What Vehicle Damage Is Covered by Insurance?

As long as you qualify to make a claim, automobile insurance will cover any accident-related damage to your vehicle. It also covers damage to any things in or on your vehicle, as long as they are not commercial goods. Common items damaged in vehicles are cell phones, eyeglasses, and laptop computers. You will need evidence to prove that these items were in fact damaged in the vehicle. Insurance companies are always suspicious of claims for damaged vehicle contents because they are easy to fake.

How to Know if you Qualify to Make a Claim

Not everyone is entitled to make a claim for vehicle damage. You only qualify if one of the following situations applies to you: 1) someone else was at fault for the damage, or 2) your auto insurance includes collision coverage.

You always qualify to make a vehicle damage claim if another person was at fault for the accident. If both your vehicle and the at-fault person's vehicle are registered in New Brunswick, then you file a claim for direct compensation for property damage (DCPD) *with your own insurance company.* If the at-fault driver's vehicle is not registered in New Brunswick (i.e., it is from another province), then you would make your property damage claim directly against the at-fault driver's insurance company.

If you were at fault for the damage to your vehicle or its contents, then you can only make an insurance claim if you have collision coverage, and the damage was accidental. Intentional damage or drinking and driving disqualify you from your insurance coverage.

Vehicle Damage Claims: Four Steps from Start to Finish

It is fairly easy to handle your property damage claim on your own. The entire process usually takes two to four weeks, but it can take longer if the at-fault person was driving a non-New Brunswick registered vehicle. Within two to four weeks, you can expect to have your vehicle repaired or to have a check issued to you for the actual cash value of your vehicle if it was damaged beyond repair. Following are the four steps from start to finish:

Step 1: Report the Accident and Vehicle Damage

If you have been involved in an accident and there is any possibility of injuries or vehicle damage, then you need to report the accident to your insurance company as soon as possible. Sometimes the other driver will offer to pay you cash for the damages in exchange for your promise not to report the accident—*you never want to do this*. Once you notify your insurance company, it will assign an adjuster to your case. The adjuster will send you the insurance claim forms.

Step 2: Submit Insurance Forms and Investigation

Once you get the insurance forms, you need to fill them out and get them back to your adjuster as soon as possible. Your adjuster will review the forms and do his or her own investigation into the accident. He or she does this by speaking with you and other witnesses and by getting the police report of the accident. It is okay for you to speak with the adjuster from your own insurance company. Your adjuster will hire collision damage experts to give quotes on the cost of repairs and the actual cash value of your vehicle.

What happens next depends on what process applies to your situation. There are three processes: the DCPD process, the collision coverage process, and the third-party claim process.

The DCPD Process

You use the direct compensation for property damage process if you believe another person was at fault for your accident, and you both were driving New Brunswick registered vehicles. Your adjuster will handle the claim for DCPD.

Your adjuster will get a quote for the "fair" value for your vehicle damage. This quote will be based on either the estimated cost to repair (if your car can be fixed) or the actual cash value of your vehicle (if it is damaged beyond repair). Once the adjuster has the quote, he or she will move on to apply the *Fault Determination Regulation* for your situation.

Under the DCPD process, insurance adjusters are required to determine fault using the fault determination diagrams found in the *Fault Determination Regulation*. These regulations set out just about every conceivable accident scenario. The insurance company will pick a fault diagram and scenario that it believes will apply to your situation.

If the scenario says you are not at fault, then the insurance company will pay the compensation based on what it determined was fair value for your vehicle damage. If the scenario says you are 50 percent at fault, then the insurance company will pay you 50 percent of what it determined was the fair value of your vehicle damage.

If you or the at-fault driver was driving a non-New Brunswick insured vehicle, then you will need to go through the third-party claim process or the collision coverage process.

Collision Coverage Process

The collision coverage process works almost exactly like the DCPD process. You make the claim directly with your insurance company. Your insurance company will do the same things as described above. *The Fault Determination Regulation* does not apply, but the adjuster will use the same principles to determine fault.

Third Party Claim Process

The third-party claim process is different because you make the claim with another person's insurance company. You will have to use the third-party claim process if the at-fault person was driving a non-New Brunswick registered vehicle, and you don't have collision coverage under your own insurance policy.

You have to put the other driver's insurance company on notice by sending them a letter or e-mail or by calling them. You can get the contact information from the police. Once the insurance company gets notice of your claim, it will do an investigation and interview of its insured driver and other witnesses. It will also want to view your vehicle to get quotes and appraisals of the damage and cost of repairs.

Third-party claims tend to be more adversarial because you are dealing with another person's insurance company. Unlike your own insurance company, the other driver's insurance company has no duty of fairness to you. Unreasonable settlement offers and lowball tactics are common. You can expect to get take-it-or-leave-it offers.

If you disagree with the insurance company's offer to you for repairs or for the actual cash value (and most likely you will), your only alternative is to file a lawsuit for vehicle damage. Usually the dispute is only over a few thousand dollars. Filing a lawsuit creates more stress and inconvenience for you. It may cost you more to fight them than what you will actually get if you win. For these reasons, many people accept the bad deal offered by the insurance company. Be smart and get collision coverage so you can avoid this mess.

Step 3: Claim Negotiation and Settlement

Once the insurance company has finished its investigation, it will either decline your claim or make a settlement offer to you. Usually the insurance company will make a settlement offer to you *based on its view* of the cost of repairs or the actual cash value of your vehicle, whichever is less. If you are satisfied with the offer from the insurance company, then you can accept it. You will have to sign forms releasing the insurance company from any further vehicle damage claims for this accident.

If you feel the insurance company's offer is too low, you can decline their offer and make a counteroffer to them. For your counteroffer to have any chance of success, you should include a letter from your own repair shop giving a quote on the cost of repairs or the actual cash value of your vehicle.

Sometimes the insurance company will pay what you ask, but more commonly, they will offer to settle for somewhere between their offer and your offer. At some point, however, the insurance company will give you a take-it-or-leave-it offer. You then have to accept it or file a lawsuit against the insurance company. Once you file a lawsuit, a judge will have the final say on the value of your property damage.

If the insurance company denies your claim, it will set out reasons, but the most common reason is because it feels you were 100 percent at fault for the collision, and you don't have collision coverage. Again, you have the option of filing a lawsuit to get a final decision from a judge.

Step 4: Trial

You have the option of filing your lawsuit for property damage in the small claims court of New Brunswick; *however, it is critical that you consult a lawyer before doing so if you have suffered any injuries in the accident and there is any possibility you may make a claim for injury compensation.*

Filing a small-claims lawsuit for property damage is a huge risk because you may lose the right to later bring a lawsuit for compensation for injuries suffered in the same accident. You need to bring both claims under the same lawsuit. The downside of this is that you may have to wait a long time to get compensation for the damage to your vehicle.

If you made the mistake of doing a small-claims lawsuit before reading this book, and the insurance company is now denying your claim for personal injury compensation for that reason, contact a lawyer for advice as soon as possible.

Disputes over "Actual Cash Value"

There is a very good chance that you will think the insurance company's offer of compensation for vehicle damage is too low. If your vehicle is

damaged beyond repair, most insurance policies only cover the "actual cash value" of your vehicle. Actual cash value is an insurance concept that means the amount your car would have sold for on the open market, in the condition it was in immediately before being damaged. There are two situations where the actual cash value often seems unfair but may actually be fair.

The first situation involves very new cars. If your car was very new, it is quite possible that the actual cash value will be less than the outstanding loan on your vehicle. This is because the value of some cars depreciates faster than you are paying off the loan. In this situation, your compensation for vehicle damage may be less than your outstanding loan amount! Understandably this gets people upset, but there is little you can do if the insurance company is offering you fair compensation.

The second situation involves older cars in great condition. Older cars and motorcycles can be in great condition, but they may have very low actual cash value. This is a problem because it may be difficult for you to find a replacement vehicle that is in as good condition as was your vehicle. If you have done custom upgrades or modifications to the vehicle or recently paid for repairs to the vehicle, it is often impossible to have these expenses reflected in the actual cash value.

In both of these situations, you will need to weigh the pros and cons of accepting the insurance company's low offer. You have to consider that they may have fairly assessed the actual cash value. Often it is not worth the time and expense to bring a lawsuit against the insurance company to seek a higher payout from them.

CHAPTER 3

Making a Claim for No-Fault Accident Benefits

In this chapter:

- description of "accident benefits"
- how to apply for accident benefits
- medical and rehabilitation expenses
- loss-of-income payments
- replacement housekeeping expenses

What Are Accident Benefits?

The law requires that all automobile insurance policies in New Brunswick include coverage for accident-related expenses and losses, including medical expenses, lost wages, housekeeping service expenses, and death/funeral expenses. These accident benefits are called no-fault benefits because anyone hurt in an accident can qualify for them, regardless of who was at fault for the accident.

You will hear lawyers or insurance adjusters refer to *section B accident benefits*. This is just a reference to the fact that these benefits are found in section B of your automobile policy.

How to Apply for Accident Benefits

Applying for accident benefits is something you can easily do on your own. You have to be organized, and there are specific things you need to do. You will need to speak with an insurance adjuster and fill out forms. Depending on what benefits you are applying for and how quickly you get the forms in, insurance companies can approve benefits in a matter of days or weeks. Following is a summary of the steps you need to follow when applying for accident benefits:

Step 1: Apply to the Right Insurance Company

There are rules covering what insurance company has to pay your accident benefits claim. The first rule is that you will always apply to an insurance company covering one of the vehicles involved in the accident (with rare exceptions). It works like this: If you were a passenger or driver of a vehicle, *then you apply to the vehicle you were in*, regardless of who was at fault for the accident and even if you are not the owner of that vehicle. If you were a pedestrian or bicyclist, then you apply to the insurance company covering the vehicle that hit you.

The police get the insurance information about all vehicles involved in the accident, and you have a right to this information. The police officer will usually write this all down on a card and give it to you at the accident scene. You can also get this information from the police station.

Step 2: Notify the Insurance Company and Get the Forms

Most insurance companies are proactive, and the company that is involved will contact you to identify itself as the accident benefits insurer. If that doesn't happen, you need to identify the right insurance company and then contact them by phone using the information you got from the police or the driver of your vehicle. In many cases, this will be your own insurance company, so you will have all the contact information.

Once you speak with the insurance company, give them the basic details of the accident and ask them to send you the *accident benefits forms*. You can also download these forms from my website: NewBrunswickCarAccidentLawyer.ca.

Step 3: Submit the Forms and Interview with Adjuster

You apply for accident benefits by filling out and submitting three forms to the insurance company. These are called the accident benefits forms. There is a form for you to fill out, a form for your doctor to fill out, and a form for your employer to fill out. The insurance company will usually not approve your claims until all the forms are submitted. A delay in submitting one form can hold up your entire application.

The insurance company will assign an adjuster to handle your accident benefits claim. The adjuster will be your contact person. You send your forms and any other expenses or receipts to him or her. The adjuster will usually want to interview you about the accident and your injuries, either by phone or in person. Technically, you have no obligation to give this interview, but it usually makes sense to do it *as long as you don't sign any written statements or allow yourself to be recorded.*

The adjuster will also ask you to sign an *authorization form for release of records*. The authorization form they give you is very broadly worded, and if you sign it, it allows the adjuster very broad power to communicate with anyone about you and to get copies of all medical records and employment records.

You never want to sign their authorization form as it gives them too much power. You should instead sign a limited authorization form, which gives them just the level of authorization they need to administer your claim but not so much that they can do damage to your case. You can download a copy of my Limited Authorization Form from my website: NewBrunswickCarAccidentLawyer.ca.

Medical and Rehabilitation Expenses Reimbursement

Accident benefits cover any vehicle accident-related medical or rehabilitation expenses that are not covered by Medicare or another insurance plan. The insurance company relies on your doctor to certify what expenses are accident related. Following is a summary of the medical and rehabilitation accident benefits and the coverage criteria:

- coverage up to $50,000 per person
- only for treatment of injuries suffered in the accident
- only for expenses "incurred" within four years of the accident
- for "reasonable and necessary" medical treatment and professional services
- for other services and supplies that are "essential" for occupational retraining or rehabilitation
- travel expenses for attending "approved" medical appointments and rehabilitation

Accident benefits insurance companies pay treatment expenses on a case-by-case basis. Following is a summary of the rules that apply to you:

- You must file your claim within thirty days.
- Your physician must recommend all treatment in writing.
- If you are covered under another health insurance plan, then you must send expenses to that plan first, before the accident benefits plan.
- You may have to pay for treatment expenses up front and then submit receipts to the accident benefits insurer for reimbursement.

- Direct payment from the insurance company to health professionals is optional for the accident benefits insurer.

Some accident benefits insurers will require you to pay up front for treatment expenses. You then submit the receipts to the accident benefits insurer for reimbursements. The turnaround time for reimbursement can be thirty to sixty days or more.

This arrangement presents problems for the vast majority of people who simply cannot afford to pay thousands of dollars in rehabilitation expenses and wait months for reimbursement. Many accident benefits insurers will agree to direct payment arrangements with your treatment providers, but this is at the discretion of the insurance company.

It also important to understand that your accident benefits are supplemental insurance—also known as "second payer" insurance. If you have medical coverage though another insurance policy or group benefits plan, then that plan is considered your primary plan or "first payer." By law, you must first put all accident-related expenses through your primary medical plan if you have one. Your "accident benefits" insurance is a secondary payer, meaning it only kicks in to pay accident-related expenses or copayments not covered by your primary medical plan. Your primary medical plan will be any medical plan you have yourself or that you are insured under (i.e., spouse's plan, or parent's plan).

You may be upset to learn that you first have to put all accident-related medical and rehabilitation expenses through your own medical plan. This is annoying and can cause problems for you for a number of reasons.

Some medical plans require you to pay for the expense and then submit the receipt for reimbursement. This means you have to find money to pay for treatment up front and then wait weeks or months to be reimbursed by your insurance company. If they only reimburse you for 80 percent (which is common), then you need to take their statement and send it to your accident benefits insurer to collect back the other 20 percent. This creates an administrative nightmare.

Another problem is that some medical plans have yearly maximum amounts per family (e.g., $1000 per year), so once you use all the coverage for your car accident injuries, there will be no coverage available for your family members until the plan refreshes again the next year.

If you don't have a private medical plan and are not covered under someone else's plan, then your accident benefits insurer will be your primary plan. This makes it easier for you to administer as you are only dealing with one insurance company. You will have a maximum coverage of $50,000 over four years.

Loss-of-Income Payments

Loss-of-income payments are one of the most important accident benefits. If you qualify, you receive up to 80 percent of your pre-accident weekly income or $250 per week, whichever is less. The most you can get is $250 per week. The benefits are calculated on a weekly basis, but they are paid to you once per month. Loss-of-income payments can be temporary, while you are off work recovering from your injuries; or payable for life, if you are permanently disabled from all forms of work.

Not everyone who is injured in a vehicle accident will qualify for weekly income payments. You can only qualify if you meet the criteria for being "employed" as defined by the insurance policy. This does not mean that you had to be in the course of your work at the time of the accident, only that you did have a job or were self-employed. If you didn't have a job at the time of the accident, there are still ways you can meet the definition of "employed." You will be considered "employed" if *any of the following situations* applies to you:

- You were actively engaged in an occupation or employment for wages or profit at the date of the accident.

- You are between the ages of eighteen and sixty-five and were employed for any six of the last twelve months leading up to the date of the accident.
- You were a seasonal worker and planned to return to employment when the season opened.
- You were scheduled to start a new job but hadn't started yet.

If your injuries will permanently disable you from doing your own occupation or job, then you can receive weekly loss-of-income payments for up to 104 weeks (e.g., two years). You will only qualify for weekly loss-of-income payments after 104 weeks if your accident-related injuries permanently disable you from doing any type of employment or work. If you are permanently disabled from all forms of employment, and you cannot be retrained to do something else, then you can receive weekly income payments for life.

Replacement Housekeeping Expenses

Accident benefits will cover replacement housekeeping services in very limited circumstances. If you qualify, the insurance company will pay $100 per week for a maximum of fifty-two weeks for replacement housekeeping services. In order to qualify, a doctor must certify that your accident-related injuries render you incapable of performing your own housekeeping, and you must not be employed. You cannot receive both replacement housekeeping services and loss-of-income payments.

CHAPTER 4

Making a Claim for Personal Injury Compensation

In this chapter:

- description of a "personal injury claim"
- how to know if you qualify to make a claim
- the types of compensation available
- how to know how much your case is worth
- personal injury claims from start to finish
- important deadlines
- understanding the burden of proof

What Is a Personal Injury Claim?

A *vehicle accident personal injury claim* is a demand you make for financial compensation for losses you suffered (or will suffer) because of injuries from a vehicle accident. These losses include accident-related financial losses (out-of-pocket expenses, lost wages, future medical costs, etc.), but they also include nonfinancial losses such as pain, suffering, and loss of enjoyment of life.

You get financial compensation for these losses by filing a lawsuit against the person or people who were at fault for your injuries. Tort law governs accident injury claims, so they are handled differently from typical insurance claims like with accident benefits. You must pursue your case as a lawsuit against the at-fault person.

How to Know If You Qualify to Make a Claim

Not everyone hurt in a motor vehicle accident is entitled to make a personal injury claim. You only qualify to make a claim if your injuries were caused by the fault of another driver or person. You make the injury claim against that person and his or her automobile insurance company. Common people who may be at fault would be the driver of the vehicle you were in or the driver of a vehicle that hit you. If you were the driver in a single-vehicle accident, then you would usually not qualify to make a claim unless there is someone else to blame for the accident (e.g., government for poor road conditions or owners of animals in the road).

The Types of Compensation Available

The law says that you are entitled to full compensation for any financial losses or expenses that were caused by injuries suffered in the vehicle accident. In theory, the at-fault person must compensate you to the point where you are no worse off financially than you would have been had the accident not happened. The law allows for specific types of compensation, which are often referred to as *heads of damages*:

- **Past loss of income:** This compensation includes lost wages or income from not being able to return to work to the extent you did before being injured.
- **Future loss of income:** This compensation is based on predictions of what you would have earned had the accident not happened, as compared to what you can now earn in your

injured condition. This claim is common if you are left with permanent disability that restricts your ability to earn income.
- **Loss of housekeeping capacity:** This compensation is based on your loss of ability to do housekeeping, yard work, and home maintenance tasks. The loss is based on the cost for you to hire replacement services to do the things you can no longer do.
- **Past and future medical expenses:** This compensation includes costs for medical expenses not covered by your accident benefits. If you have lifelong medical expenses, this compensation will pay for expenses beyond the $50,000 paid by accident benefits over four years.
- **Pain, suffering, and loss of enjoyment of life:** This compensation is not linked to any tangible expense or loss; rather, it is a payment meant to compensate you for how you have been inconvenienced by your injuries. The greater the inconvenience, the more compensation you get. The courts have imposed arbitrary limits on how much compensation you can get for pain, suffering, and loss of enjoyment of life. The upper limit is $310,000 for cases involving catastrophic injuries. Judicial decisions in New Brunswick have established guidelines for what compensation can be awarded in different circumstances.

How to Know How Much Your Case Is Worth

Everyone wants to know what his or her case is worth. I'm sure you are wondering the same thing. The most common misunderstanding people have is that personal injury cases have some preset value—this is not true. There are multiple factors that go into what your case may be worth.

In the simplest sense, your case is worth what the insurance company will agree to pay you (for out-of-court settlement) or what a judge will award you (after a trial). Understanding how courts and insurance companies value injury claims is one of the most important things you need to learn. It's perhaps the most important thing that I teach all of my clients. To know what your case is worth, you need to first understand the general principles lawyers, insurance companies, and judges use to assess compensation in personal injury cases:

1. **Compensation is not based on the type of injury.** This is a common misconception. Compensation is based on the impact the injury has on your life. Important questions are, how much disruption has it caused in your life? What are your actual wage losses? How much pain have you suffered? Is the disruption to your life temporary or permanent? Depending on the answers to these questions, the same injury can result in vastly different compensation from one person to another.

   This is because the same injury can cause different levels of disruption for people, depending on their activities and employment. For example, an amputated finger may have minimal impact on a lawyer's ability to do his or her job, but it could mean a surgeon could no longer operate on patients. The difference in compensation in the two cases could be hundreds of thousands of dollars.

2. **Your case does not have a specific value or worth.** It is impossible for anyone to quote you a specific value for your case. Personal injury cases don't work that way. It is more accurate to think of your case as having *a range of possible values* from low to high. Actually, each case has two ranges. The first range is the high and low amount of compensation a judge could give you at trial. The second range is the high and low amount of compensation that the insurance company may pay to settle your case out of court.

   As you may have guessed, the out-of-court settlement range is always lower than the range you might get at trial. Insurance companies will always offer you less than you could potentially get at trial—sometimes a lot less. For example, the trial range for your case may be $10,000 to $150,000, but the settlement range for the case may be $5,000 to $75,000.

3. **Your case has to be handled a specific way to maximize its value.** Your case has no inherent value. In other words, what your case is worth depends on how well it is put together and the amount of negotiating leverage you have against the insurance company at the time of settlement. It is easy for you—or an incompetent lawyer—to achieve a financial settlement or court award in the low end of your case's settlement range; however, it takes a lot of skill, time, and money to achieve a settlement at the high end of your case's settlement or trial range.

I am confident any experienced personal injury lawyer will tell you he or she can negotiate much higher out-of-court settlements after he or she has filed a lawsuit, hired the right experts for your case, and scheduled your case for trial. This is why the same case can settle for $5,000; $20,000; or $200,000 depending on how well it is put together. There is a saying among personal injury lawyers that the easiest way to get your first $1 million settlement is to screw up a $5 million case.

4. **It is impossible to get a quick settlement that is at the high end of your case's settlement range.** Unless you have a minor injury case, you need to dismiss any notion that your insurance company will quickly settle your case at the high end of your settlement range. Don't believe anyone who tells you otherwise, including other lawyers or insurance adjusters. This type of thinking shows a complete lack of understanding of how insurance companies operate.

It is no secret that insurance companies are for-profit organizations. The insurance company's goal is to maximize its profits by paying you the least amount of money possible. If they can pay you below fair value, their profits increase.

There is nothing wrong with you deciding to settle your case at the low end of your settlement range as long as you understand that is what you are doing. Some insurance representatives and lawyers may try to convince you that you are getting a good result by settling early—don't believe them. As a general rule, getting higher value settlements takes more time, work, and investment of money in your case. Not all lawyers can get you the same result. A lawyer who is willing to spend money on your case, file a lawsuit, and push it toward trial will be in a better position to negotiate a higher settlement.

As a general rule, you will always get low-end value when accepting a settlement before filing a lawsuit or hiring experts to prove your case. The only exception is with minor injury cases or the most severe injury cases. I believe it is possible to achieve fair value settlements early on in *some* minor injury cases. The critical thing is to make sure your case is truly a minor injury case.

Many cases will fall in a gray area of being a minor injury or non-minor injury. In those cases, it will be impossible for you to get fair value early on without gathering proper medical evidence to support your case. The insurance company will simply assert that your case is minor and offer you minor injury compensation.

5. **The courts have established ranges and limits for compensation for pain, suffering, and loss of enjoyment of life.** These ranges and limits increase each year at the rate of inflation. As of 2013, the important ranges for pain, suffering, and loss of enjoyment of life are as follows:

   a. $1 to $7,500 for "minor personal injury"
   b. $20,000 to $60,000 for chronic pain that is persistently troubling, but not totally disabling
   c. $320,000 is the maximum limit for pain, suffering, and loss of enjoyment of life

These are the ranges that you can get at trial; however, this does not mean an insurance company will ever offer you money in these ranges. For example, you may have chronic pain that you consider to be "persistently troubling, but not totally disabling" and the insurance company may offer you only the $7,500 amount for a minor injury.

6. **There are no set ranges or limits for compensation for your financial losses arising from the accident.** While the courts and provincial government have imposed arbitrary limits on compensation for pain, suffering, and loss of enjoyment of life, there are no limits or ranges of compensation for financial losses you suffer from the accident. In theory at least, you are entitled to full compensation for your financial losses arising from lost wages (past and future), replacement housekeeping services (past and future), and medical expenses (past and future). I say "in theory" because you do not get your actual financial losses, only the financial losses you can prove in court—and it is very difficult (and expensive) to prove future financial losses in court.

7. **Problems with proving liability can dramatically reduce your compensation.** As the injured person making a claim, you have the burden of proving another person was 100 percent at fault for your injuries. You and the other driver may know he or she was 100 percent at fault, but if he or she lies, can you prove it in court?

    Many people fail to gather critical evidence from the accident scene that would prove the fault of the other driver (i.e., photos of the cars, marks on the road, etc.). This type of evidence can disappear over time if you don't gather it right away. Failing to get this evidence can be a disaster, as you have no physical proof to support your allegation that the other driver was at fault. If a judge assesses your compensation to be $100,000 but then rules that the other driver was only 50 percent at fault, then you would only receive $50,000 as compensation.

8. **Problems with proving causation of injuries can dramatically reduce your compensation.** Similar to proving liability (fault of the other driver), you also have to prove that the accident caused your problems and disability. You may know with absolute certainty what injuries were caused by the accident, but can you prove it in court? *Remember, you do not get compensation based on what you know the truth to be; rather, you get compensation based on what you can prove in court.*

   If you suffered from back pain before the accident, or if you a suffered similar injuries in the past, then your case needs to be handled very carefully to make sure you receive fair compensation. A good lawyer can turn preexisting injuries and symptoms to your advantage, but only if the lawyer knows about them and hires the right experts to explain things. Hiding this information from your lawyer is one of the dumbest things you can do.

Personal Injury Claims from Start to Finish

Personal injury claims are handled differently from your accident benefits claim or vehicle damage claims. In those cases, you make the claim by submitting forms to the insurance company. You don't fill out any forms for a personal injury claim; rather, you start the claim by filing a lawsuit against the at-fault person or by giving him or her notice that you intend to do so. You can do this by sending a letter to the person or his or her insurance company. In many cases, insurance companies are proactive and will seek you out to see if you are making a claim.

Once the insurance company gets notice of your claim, it will assign an insurance adjuster to handle your claim. This adjuster will contact you, and from that point forward, you deal with the adjuster only. The adjuster investigates the merits of your intended personal injury claim. They do this by speaking with their insured driver (the at-fault person) and other witnesses. They will also want to speak with you to gather as much information from you as possible *and to influence you to do things that will hurt your case and help their case.*

The insurance adjusters will use the promise of a settlement offer as bait to lure you into the trap of agreeing to give them permission to get your medical records and to speak directly with your doctors. If you don't know what you are doing, it is a major mistake to give this power to the insurance adjuster for the at-fault driver.

From the day of the accident, you have up to two years to file a lawsuit for your case. Once your case is in the court system, you can continue to negotiate with the insurance company up to the time of trial. It is possible to settle some minor injury claims directly with the adjuster before filing a lawsuit; however, for more serious cases, you will not be able to negotiate a fair value settlement unless you file a lawsuit and gather expert evidence to support your case.

Once your case is in the court system, it goes through a series of stages. The first stage involves the exchange of all documents between you and the insurance company. The second stage, called a discovery examination, involves the insurance company's lawyer interviewing you under oath with your lawyer present. The third stage involves preparing your case for trial by gathering the final documents and reports from experts who will help prove your case.

Before trial, it is common for your case to go to a judicial settlement conference or mediation. Settlement conferences and mediations are full or half-day sessions where you meet with the insurance company to try and reach an out-of-court settlement. The final stage is a trial of your case before a judge. The judge has the final say on what compensation, if any, the insurance company must pay you.

Important Deadlines

There are several deadlines that apply to personal injury claims. In most situations, the deadline to file a lawsuit is two years from the day of the accident. There are special circumstances that may impose deadlines as short as one year. Missing a deadline is a serious problem and can result in you losing your right to compensation.

Understanding the Burden of Proof

When you file a personal injury lawsuit, you have the burden of proving the injuries and financial losses caused by the accident. A judge is required to start with the assumption that you were not in a car accident and have suffered no injuries. It is your responsibility to present enough evidence to convince the judge to accept the key facts you need to win your case, including 1) that you were involved in an accident, 2) that the other driver was at fault, 3) that you suffered injuries in the accident, 4) those injuries caused you loss of income (past or future), and 5) that you suffer permanent disability and loss of enjoyment of life.

Having the burden of proof means that if you don't present enough evidence to convince the judge to rule in your favor, then you lose, because the judge's starting point is that nothing happened or is wrong with you. This is why it is critical to preserve key evidence related to your case, such as photos of the damage to the vehicle and of the condition of the road at the accident scene.

This is why it is very important to make sure your injuries are well documented by doctors and other health professionals who see you in the days, weeks, and months after the accident. I continually tell my clients: the value of your case is not based what you know to be true; rather, *the value of your case is based on what we can prove in court.*

CHAPTER 5

"Minor Personal Injury" Claims

In this chapter:

- definition of "minor personal injury"
- what it means to suffer "serious impairment"

New Brunswick has special rules for people who have suffered a *minor personal injury* as defined by provincial insurance laws and regulations. Having a minor personal injury means you will get less compensation for pain and suffering, than you would normally get if there were no limitation imposed by regulation.

For so-called minor personal injury cases, the government has imposed an upper limit of $7,500 as compensation for pain, suffering, and loss of enjoyment of life. For example, if you would normally be entitled to $25,000 for pain, suffering, and loss of enjoyment of life, but fall under the definition of "minor personal injury," then your compensation would be decreased from $25,000 to the maximum $7,500.

The $7,500 limit for minor personal injuries increases each January at the rate of inflation.

What Is the Definition of "Minor Injury"?

For accidents happening on or after July 1, 2013, the New Brunswick Insurance Act and Injury Regulation define minor personal injury as follows:

> 4.2 (2) For the purposes of this Part and section 365.21 of the Act, "minor personal injury" means any of the following injuries, including any clinically associated sequelae, that do not result in serious impairment or in permanent serious disfigurement:
>
> (a) a contusion;
> (b) an abrasion;
> (c) a laceration;
> (d) a sprain;
> (e) a strain; and
> (f) a whiplash-associated disorder.

As a general rule, if you suffer one of the injuries listed above, then you will be deemed to have suffered a minor personal injury, *unless your injury causes you to suffer from serious impairment* or *serious disfigurement*.

If you suffer *serious impairment* or *serious disfigurement*, you are entitled to full compensation even though your injury was in the list of so-called "minor personal injuries".

What Does It Mean to Suffer "Serious Impairment"?

If you suffer one of the six listed minor personal injuries (see above), then the main issue is whether your injuries cause *serious impairment*. Proving you suffer *serious impairment* can mean the difference of tens of thousands of dollars. Let's look at what you have to prove. The definition of *serious impairment* is found at section 4.2(1) of the *Injury Regulation*:

4.2(1) "serious impairment" means, in respect of a plaintiff, an impairment of a physical or cognitive function that

(a) results in a substantial inability to perform
  (i) the essential tasks of the plaintiff's regular employment, occupation or profession, despite the plaintiff's reasonable efforts to use any accommodation provided to assist the plaintiff in performing those tasks,
  (ii) the essential tasks of the plaintiff's training or education in a program or course that the plaintiff was enrolled in or had been accepted for enrollment in at the time of the accident, despite the plaintiff's reasonable efforts to use any accommodation provided to assist the plaintiff in performing those tasks, or
  (iii) the plaintiff's normal activities of daily living,
(b) has been ongoing since the accident, and
(c) is not expected to improve substantially.

As you can see, the definition of *serious impairment* is complicated. Basically, you have to show that your injuries caused permanent symptoms that cause major problems with your work or activities outside of work. This can include major problems with your ability to keep working at the job you had before the accident. It can include major problems with returning to the education program you were enrolled in at the time of the accident. It can include major problems with doing any activities you did before the accident, including housework, yard work, home maintenance, hobbies, sports, and intimate relations with your significant other.

It is up to you to prove that the major problems are caused by accident-related injuries. The fact you have some ongoing problems with your work or activities is not enough; is has to be major problems.

If you suffer one of the listed minor personal injuries, you should expect the insurance company to automatically say you fall under the minor injury cap. They simply will not accept or believe your accident-related injuries cause serious problems for you.

In my experience, insurance companies will only pay settlements above the minor injury amount if you build a case with overwhelming evidence showing you have suffered serious impairment. It is practically impossible for you to do this without the help of a lawyer who is both experienced in car accident injury cases and who is willing to spend (at least) $4,000 to $8,000 to hire medical experts necessary to prove your case.

CHAPTER 6

Representing Yourself

In this chapter:

- educate yourself
- negotiating a settlement on your own
- why you may need a lawyer to get a fair value settlement
- three things to consider for minor-injury settlements

Even if you plan to hire a lawyer, there will be a period of time when you represent yourself in your own vehicle accident case. At minimum, you will need to represent yourself early on in the days, weeks, and months following your accident. The choices you make during this time matter, and they can have long-term repercussions for your case (both good and bad). In this chapter, I review some of the basic things you should know and do when handling your own claim.

Educate Yourself

It is critical that you educate yourself as soon as possible about how the car accident claim system works. The fact that you are reading this book means you are already on your way to learning what you need to know. This book is meant to give you basic background knowledge of how vehicle accident cases work in New Brunswick.

Negotiating a Settlement on Your Own

In my experience, not everyone needs a lawyer to settle a car accident injury case for good value. For example, if you are only dealing with a claim for property damage or if you suffered very minor injuries, then it is possible for you to get the insurance company to make a reasonable settlement offer to you. It will take some work and self-study on your part, but you can do it.

On the other hand, if your injuries do not completely heal, and you are left with ongoing problems that interfere with your ability to work or your ability to do daily activities, then you need to seriously consider hiring a lawyer to represent you if you want more than a low-end settlement for your case.

Do not be naive and believe that you can negotiate a fair settlement for a serious injury case on your own without filing a lawsuit and without hiring experts to support your case. Some insurance companies—or even some incompetent lawyers—may try to convince you that you can. You can't. Insurance settlements don't work that way, and any experienced personal injury lawyer or honest insurance representative will tell you so.

In more serious cases, you will need to do certain things to cause the insurance company to make a reasonable settlement offer to you. These things include filing a lawsuit, gathering evidence to prove your case, paying for copies of medical records, hiring experts to prove certain parts of your case, and knowing how to maximize negotiating leverage with the insurance company. It is conceivable that with enough time, self-study, and resources, you could learn to do these things on your own, but this is impractical and unwise for the vast majority of people.

Why You May Need a Lawyer to Get a Fair Value Settlement

Why do you need a lawyer to get a settlement in the middle to upper end of your case's settlement range? One reason: leverage, or more accurately, your lack of leverage. In negotiations, leverage is a measure of which side, at any given moment, has a greater ability to influence the other side. Simply put, when you negotiate on your own without a lawyer, the insurance company has all the leverage. Once you realize this, you will understand why it is naive to believe you can convince an insurance company to pay you fair value for a serious injury case without you filing a lawsuit or hiring experts to prove your case.

Insurance companies are for-profit businesses whose only concern is maximizing profits. Executives and employees are incentivized to maximize profits. One way an insurance company maximizes its profits is by minimizing what it pays for each injury claim.

Your insurance company's goal is not to settle your case for fair value; *rather, its goal is to settle your case for the least amount of money that you will accept.* Read that sentence again, because that is really the key to success in settlement negotiations with an insurance company. Until you are able to gain leverage in the negotiations, the insurance company will start with a lowball offer and make small increases until it can get you to accept a deal. The insurance company hopes you will take a low offer because you don't think they will pay more (but they will).

I often use the following example to help my clients understand how insurance companies negotiate. Picture yourself sitting across the table from the insurance company representative. He has a handful of cash hidden out of sight and under the table. You have no idea how much he has (but *he* does). As you negotiate, he reaches under the table to take a $5 bill to place on the table, then another, then maybe a $10 bill. He knows you are entitled to the entire handful of cash, but he continues to place bills on the table slowly, hoping you will eventually accept the deal either out of frustration, financial hardship, or because you naively believe he has put all his money on the table.

Until you get leverage over the insurance company, this is how negotiations will go. Filing a lawsuit is the single best way to immediately start to get leverage over the insurance company. Our court system is the one place where you can have equal power with the insurance company—and insurance companies hate it.

The insurance company doesn't have to do what you say, but it does have to do what the court says. As long as your case is actually moving toward trial, and you continue to build your case to win at trial, you gain leverage over the insurance company. The insurance company now has to start spending money to defend against your case. If your case is prepared properly, the insurance company knows a judge will order it to pay a fair value for the case. All of a sudden, you now have the leverage in the negotiations, and it makes financial sense for the insurance company to make fair value offers to you.

Three Things to Consider for Minor-Injury Settlements

If you decide to handle your own settlement negotiations, there will eventually come a point where the insurance company gives you its final take-it-or-leave-it offer. The insurance adjuster will be adamant that your case "clearly falls under the minor injury cap." Often, this offer will be in the range of $5,000 to $7,500, which is essentially the upper limit of the minor injury cap. Before you accept this offer, you need to carefully consider the following three things:

Are You 100-Percent Sure You Only Have a Minor Personal Injury?

If you are going to settle your case for minor-injury value, then you had better be certain that you actually suffered a minor injury as defined by the laws and regulations. This may seem like a no-brainer, but I have represented many people who came to me convinced (wrongfully) that their case fell under the minor injury cap. This happens because people draw the wrong conclusions after doing their own online research or because someone in a position of authority has told them they suffered a minor injury. This someone is usually a friend, an insurance representative, a doctor, or sometimes even a lawyer.

The definition of *minor injury* is very complicated, and unless you have had a full recovery with no ongoing problems whatsoever, then there are lots of creative ways to prove that you do not fall under the definition of "minor injury." The difference in settlement value can be tens of thousands of dollars.

Are You Certain You Won't Get Worse in the Future?

Settling a case too soon is a common mistake made by self-represented people. You may assume you will get better, or you may not know the full extent of your injuries. This is why many insurance companies try to reach quick settlements with people before they get educated and before the full extent of their injuries is known.

In my opinion, you should wait a minimum of one year from the date of your accident before agreeing to settle your injury claim. Injury claim settlements are final. You can't go back for more money if you later learn you accepted a bad deal. It is very rare for a judge to overturn a bad settlement, although that has happened in a few cases. Don't put yourself in that position; do your settlement right the first time.

Does Your Medical Insurance Plan Have a Subrogated Claim?

Failing to account for subrogated claims in settlements is also a very common mistake made by self-represented people. If other insurance companies have paid benefits to you for your accident-related injuries, then those insurance companies are entitled to be reimbursed by the automobile accident insurance company.

For example, let's say that your Medavie Blue Cross medical plan paid for $5,000 of physiotherapy and medications. Under the terms of your insurance policy with Medavie Blue Cross, you are legally required to include any amounts they paid you, as part of the compensation you seek in your car accident injury claim.

In this example, you would need to seek an extra $5,000 on top of whatever the automobile insurance company wants to pay you for your minor personal injuries. These reimbursement claims from other insurance companies are called *subrogated claims*.

The automobile insurance companies know they are liable to pay subrogated claims, but they are happy to look the other way if you forget to ask for it or don't realize you are supposed to do so. There are many ethical adjusters who will point this out to you, but some will not do so.

If the adjuster offers you $8,000 as a minor personal injury settlement, and you have a subrogated claims for $5,000, then he or she should really be offering you $13,000 ($8,000 + $5,000 subrogated claim). When you receive the $13,000 settlement, you then pay the $5,000 Medavie Blue Cross, leaving you with $8,000 for yourself.

What happens if you forget to collect the extra $5,000? Simple. It comes out of your settlement funds. You are liable to pay this money even if you didn't know you had to collect it. So you will need to pay $5,000 out of your settlement funds to pay back the subrogated claim. The $8,000 settlement you thought you were getting will be reduced to $3,000 ($8,000 - $5000 subrogate claim).

This mistake usually does not come to light until several months or years after you reach a settlement of your car accident injury claim. Settlements are final, so you can't go back to ask the automobile insurance company to pay these subrogated claims, even though they were legally required to pay them.

CHAPTER 7

The Ten Things You Must Do in the First Two Weeks after Your Accident

What you do (or don't do) in the weeks after your accident will have permanent implications for your case—either good or bad, and sometimes really bad. If your goal is to protect your own interests and to build a strong foundation for your case, then there are ten things you must do within the first two weeks after your accident.

1. Have a Doctor Examine You As Soon As Possible

I cannot overstate how important it is for you to be examined by a doctor immediately after the accident. There two reasons why this is so important. First, the sooner you see a doctor, the sooner you can start receiving necessary medical care and rehabilitation for your injuries. Research shows that the sooner you start rehabilitation, the greater chance you have of getting a better recovery from your injuries. Therefore, by seeking out medical care right away, you will prevent the insurance company from later arguing that you didn't do everything possible to get better.

Second, in almost all cases, the insurance company will argue that you are exaggerating or lying about the extent of your injuries. To defend against this type of attack, you must have a doctor record details about your injuries and his or her observations as soon as possible. When a doctor examines you after an accident, he or she will make notes about such things as the details of the accident, the symptoms you are complaining about, and bruising, swelling, and other observable signs of injury. The doctor's medical records will become important later on as proof that you are not exaggerating your injuries.

2. Educate Yourself about How Vehicle Accident Cases Work in New Brunswick

I also cannot overemphasize how important it is for you to educate yourself about how vehicle accident cases work in New Brunswick. It is only by educating yourself that you can make the right choices to protect your interests and to avoid traps and mistakes that will cause permanent damage to your case. Understanding how the system works will enable you to make the right choices. The insurance company sees the first few weeks after an accident as its golden opportunity to minimize the settlement it will eventually have to pay to you. *It does this by helping you to make critical mistakes that cannot be later undone by a lawyer.*

Most people make mistakes because of a lack of understanding of the true motives of the insurance adjusters and how the system really works. A lack of understanding means you are more likely to do things against your own interests, such as giving written or recorded statements, signing forms, not bothering to collect key physical evidence, and allowing the insurance company to contact your employer or doctor.

The insurance company knows if it can get to you before you speak with a lawyer, it can build a rapport with you and lull you into a sense of false comfort and hopefully delay you in getting a lawyer for as long as possible. The longer the insurance company can keep you uninformed and not represented by a lawyer, the longer it has to build a case against you.

3. Notify Your Insurance Company If Your Vehicle Was in an Accident

You need to notify your own automobile insurance company that your vehicle was in an accident. You need to tell them details about the day, time, and location of the accident. They will want details about how the accident happened. If your vehicle was damaged or if you suffered injuries, then you need to ask for the forms to make claims for property damage and accident benefits. The insurance company will assign two representatives (also called adjusters) to contact you. One will deal with your property damage claim, and the other will deal with your accident benefits claim.

4. Take Photographs of Your Injuries

Take photos or video of all your injuries, including any cuts, scrapes, and bruises. You need to do this within the first week following the accident (or as soon as possible). Even though the cuts, scrapes, and bruises will heal, it is important to show the areas of injury, as you may have internal injuries to nerves, bones, ligaments, and other tissues that result in long-term injuries.

Insurance companies will try to say that your medical problems or symptoms are not caused by the accident. This becomes hard for them to do if you have photos or video showing your areas of injury.

5. Take Video and Photographs of the Scene of the Accident

Gathering evidence from the scene of the accident is one of the most important, yet often overlooked, parts of your case. Gathering evidence involves taking extensive photographs and video of the accident scene and surroundings. You must take photos and video as soon as possible because the roadway may change, the surroundings may change, and the physical evidence will fade or disappear over time.

If you go to the scene of the accident a few days after the event, there will usually still be a lot of physical evidence, which can include skid marks, fresh scrapes on the pavement, marks on the gravel shoulder, glass, pieces of the vehicles, and paint marks made by police investigators. You want to take many photos and video of all these things. As the days go by, the marks begin to fade, debris gets swept way, and you can't tell the accident-related scrapes from ones that were already there. The road or surroundings can change because of construction. If you wait too long, the accident-scene evidence will literally disappear.

Don't make the mistake of believing you don't need to take photos and video because the other driver has accepted fault for the accident. No matter what the driver or his or her insurance company have led you to believe, they will likely change their story by the time you file a lawsuit. If you haven't already gathered accident-scene evidence, it may no longer exist.

6. Take Videos and Photographs of All Vehicles Involved in the Accident

It is very important to take video and photographs of all vehicles involved in the accident. You want images and video of the entire vehicle and not just the damaged parts. Take special care to note the condition of the tires on all the vehicles. Bald or worn tires are often a factor in car accidents. If the tires look worn, take extensive photos and video of them, including measurements of the tread depth. You have a very short window of time to get these photos because the vehicles will be repaired or sent to the scrap yard in a matter of days or weeks after an accident.

7. Get the "Black Box" Data from the Negligent Driver's Vehicle

Most modern vehicles have *black box data recorders* that record the vehicle's speed, acceleration, and deceleration in the seconds leading up to an accident. As you can imagine, this type of evidence can be absolutely critical to winning your case. You will need to hire an accident scene investigator to gather and interpret black box data for you. The other driver or insurance company may not voluntarily give you access to this data, so you may need to get a court order to get it.

8. If Your Injuries Are Very Serious or Catastrophic, You May Need to Hire an Accident Reconstruction Expert Immediately

In cases of very serious injuries, it is almost always in your best interests to hire a professional accident-scene reconstruction expert to gather all evidence from the accident scene and vehicles. Accident-scene reconstruction experts are trained to know what to look for and can reconstruct what happened based on the physical evidence and witness testimony.

The more serious your injuries, the harder the insurance company will work to convince a judge that you should be found partially at fault for your injuries. This is because when you are found to be partially at fault, your compensation is reduced in proportion to your fault. For example, if your compensation is $1,000,000, but the insurance company convinces a judge that you were 25 percent at fault, then your compensation would be reduced to $750,000, and the insurance company would save $250,000.

Hiring an accident reconstruction expert immediately after an accident can reduce or eliminate the chances that the insurance company can convince a judge you should be partially to blame for the accident.

9. Apply for Short-Term Income Loss Payments

If there is any possibility that your injuries will keep you off work for more than two weeks, then you need to take steps to apply for weekly income loss benefits. Section B weekly income loss benefits, and employment insurance sickness benefits are the most common sources of weekly income loss payments. You need to apply to both of them at the same time.

Section B weekly income loss payments are part of your accident benefits, so you get the forms from your own automobile insurance company. EI sickness benefits are provided by Service Canada. You can download the forms online or can get them at any Service Canada location. With both section B weekly income payments, and EI sickness benefits, there are forms to be signed by you, your employer, and your doctor. If you have paid sick days available through your employment, you must use these up before you can qualify for income loss payments.

10. Advise the Other Driver's Insurance Adjuster That You Are Not Ready to Give a Statement at This Time

It is very common for the at-fault driver's insurance company to reach out to you in the days and weeks following the accident. They will usually do this by calling you on the phone or by sending you a letter by mail. They will ask if they can speak with you so they can learn more about your case.

You should politely tell them that you plan to make an injury claim, but you are not ready to meet with them or to answer any questions at this time. Tell them you want to wait for things to settle down so that you can have a better idea about the extent of your injuries before you speak with them. Don't give any information to the other driver's insurance company until you have thoroughly educated yourself and sought advice from a lawyer.

CHAPTER 8

Ten Mistakes That Will Ruin Your Injury Claim

You may believe—as many people do—that if you are honest and legitimately hurt, then you can do no wrong in handling your own injury claim. Please believe me when I say you can definitely do things to hurt your case, even if you are honest, legitimately hurt, and well meaning.

Never forget that you are dealing with a very sophisticated adversary whose overriding goal is to pay you as little money as possible. The insurance company has every incentive to do things that will undermine your case, and more importantly, it will encourage *you* to do things that will hurt your own case.

There are ten common mistakes that I see people make over and over. If you can avoid these mistakes, then you will give yourself a much better chance of getting fair compensation for your case.

1. Not Taking Time to Educate Yourself about the Car Accident Injury Claims System

I know I sound like a broken record, but I truly believe that not taking time to educate yourself is the worst mistake you can make. You can easily avoid the other nine mistakes in this list if you simply take time to learn about how car accident claims work in New Brunswick. The sooner you educate yourself, the better.

You need to have a basic idea of how the system works before you speak with insurance representatives, before you sign any forms, and before you hire a lawyer. You can educate yourself by reading books like this one, reading online blogs, attending educational seminars or webinars, or through free consultations with lawyers.

2. Giving Written or Recorded Statements to the At-Fault Driver's Insurance Adjuster

In the context of vehicle accident cases, a "statement" refers to written or tape-recorded testimony from a witness answering questions about the accident. I often receive urgent phone calls and e-mails from people who have an appointment to give a statement to the at-fault driver's insurance company later that day or within a few days.

My answer is always the same: cancel the meeting and don't give the statement. You have absolutely no obligation to give a statement. Giving verbal or written statements early on in a case *never* helps you. The best-case scenario is that the statement will be neutral. More likely it will be harmful to your case, and in the worst-case scenario, it will destroy your case.

Why is it such a bad idea to give a statement to the at-fault driver's adjuster in the first few weeks following the accident? You really are not in the right frame of mind to give a statement soon after the accident. You are vulnerable during this time because you are dealing with injuries, your life is in chaos, you will not know what story the at-fault driver is telling his insurance company, and you are less likely to be informed about your rights.

When you are in this state, it is much easier for the insurance company to ask questions that skew your answers in a way that helps them and hurts you. You are more likely to forget important information. You are more likely to just sign the written statement without reading it over to make sure the insurance representative has worded things properly. I see these same mistakes all the time.

3. Failing to Secure Evidence from the Vehicles and Accident Scene

I have seen more than one winnable case go down the drain because the injured person did not bother to take any photos of the accident scene or of the damage to the vehicles. There is absolutely no excuse not to take photos and video of the vehicles and accident scene, but many people don't bother to do so. Either they don't know they should, or they don't think they need to because the other drivers "admitted" fault at the accident scene. But these drivers often take back the admission several months later after it is too late for you to gather evidence.

If you wait several months or a year to hire a lawyer, it may be too late to go back and get photos of the accident scene and the damage to the vehicles. Marks on the road will have faded, and the vehicles will be repaired or destroyed.

Sometimes the key to winning your case will be the data contained in the so-called black box of your car or the other driver's car. This black box records things like speed, acceleration, and deceleration. You need to secure the vehicle black-box data within days or weeks of the accident, or it could be destroyed or overwritten.

4. Allowing the Insurance Company to Contact Your Doctor

Giving the insurance company permission to contact your doctor is one of the dumbest things you can do. In doing so, you make it easy for the adjuster to build a strong case against you. By framing questions in a certain way, the adjuster can lead your doctor to say things that help the insurance company and hurt you. Most doctors are busy with their day-to-day practice and do not realize they are being manipulated by the adjuster.

5. Not Seeing a Doctor Soon Enough

Not seeing a doctor immediately after an accident is a big mistake. Every day you wait, you make it easier for the insurance company to convince a judge that you weren't hurt that bad or are exaggerating your injuries. It is important to have a doctor examine and document your injuries as soon as possible, while the swelling is still there and before your cuts and bruises heal. In a few weeks, after all your superficial injuries have healed, there may be no objective signs that you were even hurt in a car accident.

Seeing a doctor earlier also means you can get started sooner with your rehabilitation. This is very important. Delays in starting rehabilitation, even for a few weeks, will raise red flags with the insurance company and with the judge. It will open the door for them to try and blame your problems on some other injury that "must have happened" after the car accident.

6. Trying to Hide or Downplay Previous Injuries or Accidents

Trying to hide or downplay previous injuries or accidents will always backfire on you. You will be exposed at some point, and when you are, your credibility will be lost—and your case long with it. If you are *my* client, you will also soon be without a lawyer, as I always fire clients who I discover have mislead me in any way.

The insurance company will eventually see every medical file and report written about you, every worker's compensation file, and other government records. Insurance companies have access to databases that tell them if you have ever been in a car accident before, so don't try to hide it.

Hiding preexisting injuries or accidents from your own lawyer is just plain stupid. A good lawyer will be able to use past injuries or accidents to your advantage. This is because many doctors will say that someone who has been injured in the past is more vulnerable to worse injuries the second time around. Having preexisting injuries can help explain why you didn't recover as expected or why you continue to suffer from pain.

7. Not Giving a Full Effort with Recommended Rehabilitation

Every so often I meet a person who resists the treatment and rehabilitation recommendations of his or her doctors or health professionals. This can include being difficult with the health professionals, missing appointments, and giving less than 100-percent effort during rehabilitation. Not giving a full effort just because you think the therapy isn't working is one of the dumbest things you can do. Insurance companies love it when people do this, because they know a judge will punish you for this type of attitude.

You have a legal duty to do everything possible to mitigate your financial losses arising from the accident. This includes giving a full effort with your rehabilitation, even if you personally feel it is not working. Judges do not like it when injured people do not give a full effort at rehabilitation. The judge will reduce your compensation by up to 50 percent if he or she believes you didn't give a full effort with your rehabilitation.

8. Not Doing Everything Possible to Return to the Workforce

The single best thing you can do to help your case and to increase the amount of compensation you get is to do everything possible to get back to the workforce in some capacity. Many people come to me with the mistaken belief that trying to get back to work will somehow hurt their case. This is a myth, and it is wrong.

Any experienced personal injury lawyer will tell you that trying to get back to work is the best thing you can do to help your case. It doesn't matter if you are successful in finding or keeping employment, simply working hard to try and keep working will impress the insurance company and the judge that decides your case. Insurance companies will actually pay more to people who are seen to be hard workers. They do this because they know a judge will also pay more compensation to such a person.

9. Misrepresenting Your Activity Level

The more serious you are hurt, the more likely it is that the insurance company will do surveillance on you. This surveillance will include online searching of your social media accounts and undercover video surveillance of you outside your house and in the community. If you are off work for more than a year, it is almost guaranteed the insurance company will get video surveillance of you.

If you are self-represented, a favorite trick of the insurance company is to call you for an interview or to send you an activity report form after they get surveillance of you doing certain activities. They are hoping that you will say something in the interview or indicate something on the activity form that they can say is inconsistent with what is shown on the video. This way, they can make you out to be a liar and a faker. Many well-meaning people fall into this trap.

10. Waiting until the Last Minute to Hire a Lawyer and File Your Lawsuit

You have two years to file a lawsuit in New Brunswick, so there is no excuse for waiting until the last minute to do so. This often happens when a self-represented person continues to try and negotiate with the insurance company right up to the two-year deadline. This is a mistake, because if you do not reach a settlement, you will be scrambling to find a lawyer to file the lawsuit before the deadline. Waiting until the last minute to file your lawsuit will greatly limit the number of lawyers who would be willing to take you on as a client. Most good lawyers are busy and will turn you away.

CHAPTER 9

Common Scenarios: What You Need to Do

Following are some fictitious scenarios to help you understand how everything fits together. Your situation will not be exactly like these examples, so you should always get specific legal advice for your situation.

Example 1: Two-Vehicle Accident, You Are the Driver and Owner of Your Vehicle

You are driving on the Trans-Canada highway and stop in a line of traffic because of construction. Paul is driving behind you and is using his cell phone to text a message. Paul doesn't realize you stopped, and the front of his car collides with the rear of your car, causing extensive damage. Both you and Paul suffer serious injuries because of the collision. You both need rehabilitation and have to be off work for the next three to six months because of your injuries.

Paul is 100 percent at fault for the collision. Your insurance company is ACME Insurance, and Paul's insurance is Allprovince Insurance. Both your vehicle and Paul's vehicle are registered in New Brunswick.

I will review the claims that you and Paul can make in this situation.

Vehicle Damage Claim

You would make your vehicle damage claim with your own insurance company (ACME Insurance). This would be a direct compensation for property damage (DCPD) claim because the other driver (Paul) is at fault, and both vehicles are registered in New Brunswick. ACME Insurance assigns an adjuster to manage your DCPD claim.

Paul's vehicle was also damaged. He has collision coverage under his own policy, so he is able to file a vehicle damage claim with Allprovince Insurance, even though he was at fault for the accident.

No-Fault Accident Benefits

You would apply for no-fault accident benefits though ACME Insurance, even though Paul was at fault for the accident. ACME Insurance will assign an adjuster to manage your claim. He or she will send you the forms. You want to apply for medical coverage for rehabilitation and weekly loss-of-income payments. Once approved, ACME Insurance will pay for 100 percent of your rehabilitation expenses and up to $250 per week for loss-of-income payments.

Paul has the right to apply for no-fault accident benefits through his own insurance company (Allprovince Insurance), even though he was at fault for the accident. Paul is entitled to the same no-fault benefits as you. He also is approved for coverage for rehabilitation and loss of income payments for up to $250 per week.

Personal Injury Claim

Since you suffered injuries because of Paul's negligence, you have the right to bring a personal injury claim against him. You would do this by notifying Paul and Allprovince of your intention to make an injury claim. At that point, Allprovince will assign a claim number to you and will take over all communications with you. You don't deal with Paul.

You then have up to two years to reach a settlement with Allprovince, or you have to file a lawsuit against Paul to protect your right to compensation. After you start the lawsuit, you can continue to negotiate with Allprovince right up to the time of trial. Many cases settle before trial, but if not, then a judge would determine your compensation. Allprovince would represent and defend Paul at the trial.

Paul also suffered serious injuries, but he is not eligible to make a personal injury claim because he was at fault for the accident.

Example 2: Two-Vehicle Accident, You Are a Passenger in a Friend's Vehicle

You are a passenger with Judy in her car. You are driving on Union Street in Saint John. Judy is in a rush to get home and is speeding. A truck coming in the opposite direction makes a left turn across your lane to head toward King's Square. Judy hits the brakes, but she still collides with the passenger side of the truck.

Randy (the driver of the truck) tells the police that the road was clear when he started his turn and that Judy "came out of nowhere!" Everyone suffers injuries in the accident, and both vehicles are damaged. Judy has insurance through ACME Insurance, and Randy has insurance with Allprovince Insurance. The police say the fault was 50/50 between Judy and Randy, even though Judy disagrees.

Vehicle Damage Claim

You did not own a vehicle involved in the accident, so you would not have a right to make a vehicle damage claim. Both Judy and Randy can make DCPD claims, but each insurance company will assess the degree of fault for both drivers.

No-Fault Accident Benefits

As a passenger, you would file your no-fault benefits claim with Judy's insurance company (ACME Insurance). Judy and Randy would each file their no-fault claims with their own insurance company.

Personal Injury Claim

In a case like this where it is possible that the fault could be split between the two drivers, you would want to file a personal injury claim against both Judy and Randy. You should notify both Allprovince Insurance and ACME Insurance that you intend to make a claim.

Example 3: Pedestrian Hit by Vehicle

You are a pedestrian crossing Mountain Road in Moncton. Phil is driving on Mountain Road and looks over at some people on the sidewalk. As he does this, he does not see you in the crosswalk and runs into you. You suffer very serious injuries. Phil has insurance with ACME Insurance. You own a car and have insurance with Allprovince.

Vehicle Damage Claim

You did not own a vehicle involved in the accident, so you would not have a right to make a vehicle damage claim. Phil does not have collision coverage with his own insurance, so he can't make a claim for vehicle damage.

No-Fault Accident Benefits

As a pedestrian, you would file your no-fault benefits claim with Phil's insurance company (ACME Insurance), even though you have your own car insurance with Allprovince. Phil also has the right to file a no-fault accident benefits claim with ACME. You are both entitled to the same accident benefits.

Personal Injury Claim

You would file a personal injury claim against Phil. You would inform Phil and ACME Insurance of your intention to do so. You then have two years to file a lawsuit for compensation. You can negotiate directly with ACME to try and reach an out-of-court settlement.

www.ingramcontent.com/pod-product-compliance
Ingram Content Group UK Ltd.
Pitfield, Milton Keynes, MK11 3LW, UK
UKHW041959230426
12048UKWH00008B/416